Survival Guides You Didn't Know You Needed

SURVIVING A SHIPWRECK AT SEA

Thomas Kingsley Troupe

BLACK RABBIT BOOKS

Hi Jinx is published by Black Rabbit Books
P.O. Box 3263, Mankato, Minnesota, 56002.
www.blackrabbitbooks.com

Marysa Storm, editor; Michael Sellner, designer;
Catherine Cates, production designer;
Omay Ayres, photo researcher

Cataloging-in-Publication Data is available at the Library of Congress.
ISBN 978-1-68072-343-4 (library binding)
ISBN 978-1-68072-373-1 (e-book)

Printed in China. 9/17

Image Credits

BDN Maine: Steve Callahan, 20 (photo); iStock: Clairevas, 8 (splashes); Darumo, 8 (suitcase); daveturton, 7 (shark); lolong, Cover (bttm kid), 4 (bttm kid); orensila, 8 (tie); Shutterstock: andryuha1981, 18 (tentacles); anfisa focusova, 12 (bkgd); Arcady, 3 (note), 6 (note); braingraph, 1 (shark); chaika, 21 (starfish); Christos Georghiou, 16 (dolphin); Cory Thoman, 11 (blck swirls); Danilo Sanino, 7 (fish, water), 11 (kid); dedMazay, 8 (white shirt); designer_an, 8 (waves), 11 (bkgd); Dualororua, 11 (photo, ray); frescomovie, Back Cover (bkgd); Freud, 13 (lifesaver), 18 (lifesaver); GN ILLUSTRATOR, 8 (fins); IADA, 21 (bkgd); Ilya Chalyuk, 5, 9 (marker strokes), 13 (marker strokes), 17, 20 (marker strokes); Klara Viskova, Cover (shipwreck), 4 (shipwreck); Lorelyn Medina, 3 (bkgd); Maciej Es, 18–19 (ship, bkgd); M.Stasy, 3 (lifesaver); Memo Angeles, 8 (boy), 12 (shark), 13 (girl, smile, magnifying glass), 16 (kid); Moriz, 18 (boy); Nearbirds, 14–15 (underwater scene); opicobello, 6 (torn paper), 12 (marker), 14 (torn paper); Pakso Maksim, Back Cover (top); 9 (torn paper), 15 (torn paper), 23 (torn paper), 24; pitju, 21 (curled corner); Ron Leishman, Cover (top kid), 4 (top kid); SlipFloat, 20 (shark); Suchkova Anna, 8 (pink shirt); Sujono sujono, 1 (octopus), 11 (octopus); Teguh Mujiono, 14–15 (fins), 23 (shark); totallypic, 20 (arrow); zooco, 11 (orange fish), 12 (eyes) Every effort has been made to contact copyright holders for material reproduced in this book. Any omissions will be rectified in subsequent printings if notice is given to the publisher.

CONTENTS

Dear Reader,

To be honest, the author's **manuscript** wasn't supposed to become a book. There was a horrible mix up. You can keep reading, if you want. Just don't take any of these suggestions seriously.

Sincerely,
a very sorry editor

Chapter 1
A CRUISE GONE WRONG

Water splashes as the cruise ship cuts through the waves. The ship sways slightly in the ocean. The smell of salt tingles your nose.

Suddenly, alarms sound. Whoa! Was that an explosion? There's a giant hole in the front of the ship. The ship's taking on water!

It could happen, you know. A ship could sink at any time.*

**Editor's Note: Well, I guess it can. But it's highly unlikely.*

Time to Survive!

Being **stranded** out at sea is no joke. Water is everywhere. There's no land in sight. Survival will be tricky.

Thankfully, you're prepared. You've got a survival guide you never thought you'd need. It's time to survive being shipwrecked at sea!*

Famous Shipwrecks in History

RMS *Titanic* (hit an iceberg)

RMS *Republic* (ran into the SS *Florida*)

RMS *Lusitania* (hit by a **torpedo**)

*Editor's Note: If you are on a sinking ship, grab an emergency kit. Just leave this book behind.

Chapter 2

STAYING AFLOAT AND ALIVE

The ship may be sinking. But that doesn't mean everything onboard will sink too. Work quickly to find objects that float. Use rope and some imagination to build a **raft**.

Don't know what'll float? Try a suitcase or an air mattress. Some breads will even float for a while. The best part? You'll have a snack on your new ship!

Survival List: Things on a Ship that Can Float

ice (Just grab some from a cooler.)
rubber duckies (You remembered to bring yours, right?)
plastic bottles (Use empty milk or soda bottles.)

Tread Water

Making a raft won't always work. There might not be enough things that float. Perhaps you're not good at building. Or maybe you ate too much of the bread.

In that case, you'll have to go back to basics. Use your swimming skills. You'll have to **tread** water. This will keep you from drowning. It's great exercise too!

According to a record book, the most time spent treading water is 85 hours.

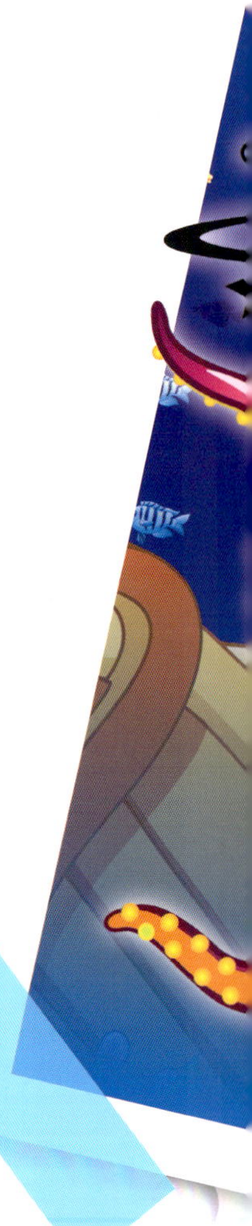

Survival List

Other Things that Could Reflect Light

a watch with a glass face
shiny steel from a sunken boat
someone's bald head

Chapter 3

GET HELP!

You wouldn't think of it during a shipwreck, but mirrors are helpful. They have many uses out at sea. Pull them out of the sinking ship's bathrooms. Then use them to reflect light at passing ships or aircraft. Blind an attacking shark!* Or make sure your teeth are clean.

**Editor's Note:* This is just silly.*

Find Atlantis

The lost island of Atlantis is **rumored** to be somewhere underwater. Use this chance to find it! Simply dive beneath the surface. Then take a look around.*

If you find Atlantis, ask someone living there for help. Mermen and mermaids are great swimmers. They might appreciate your company too.

**Editor's Note: This is a horrible suggestion. No one knows if Atlantis was even real.*

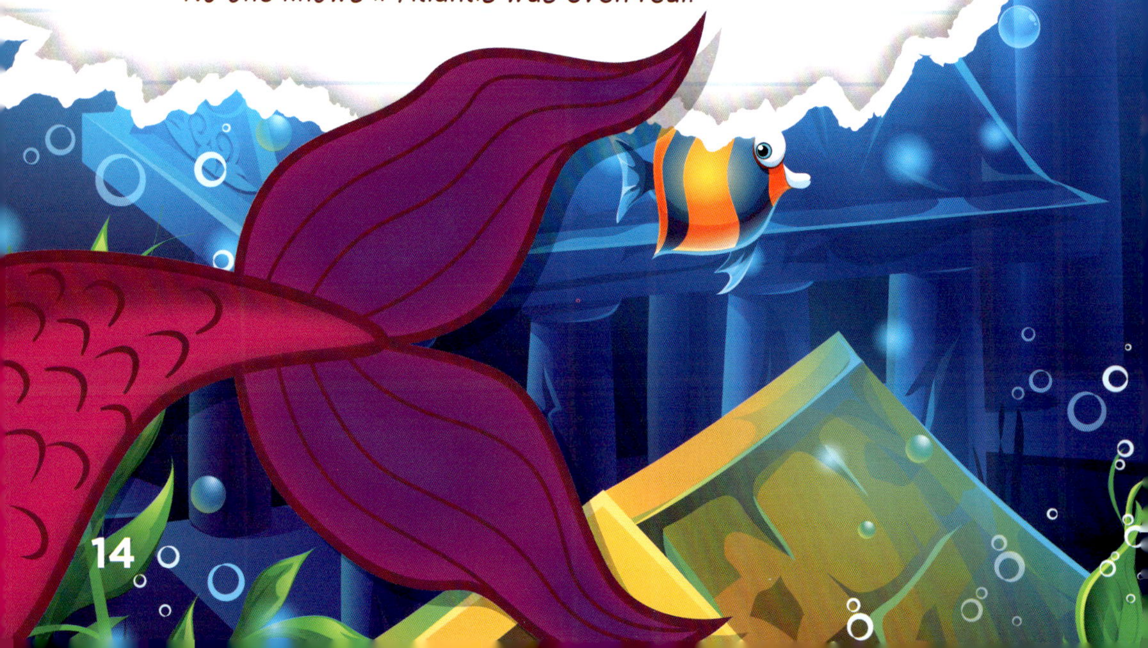

Some people think
aliens lived on Atlantis.

Chapter 4
ESCAPE THE SEA

Dolphin experts say the animals are smart. Other experts say dolphins like cash and gifts. See some dolphins? Then crack open your wallet or purse.

Dolphins will help humans. But they'll only do it for a price. Make them an offer they can't refuse. If they accept, you'll be on your way home!*

**Editor's Note: Dolphins are smart, but that's the only thing the author got right here.*

Hitch a Ride

If worse comes to worst, you can always hitch a ride. Simply stick your thumb out. Then wait for the magic to happen. If you're lucky, a ship's crew will see you. Be sure to thank the captain for the ride.*

Let's face it. You never know when you'll end up shipwrecked. It could be three months from tomorrow or later this afternoon. But with this guide, you can keep your head above water.

**Editor's Note: Oceans are huge. You could go months without seeing a ship. This idea is ridiculous.*

Chapter 5
GET IN ON THE HI JINX

It's fun to joke about being shipwrecked. But it does happen in real life. In 1982, Steve Callahan sailed **solo** across the Atlantic Ocean. On the return trip, his boat sank. Callahan escaped on a life raft with a few supplies. He drifted in the ocean for 76 days before being rescued.

Take It One Step More

1. Much of the ocean hasn't been explored. Do you think it's important that it is explored? Why or why not?

2. The ocean is full of all kinds of animals. Do some research to discover the most dangerous sea creatures.

3. What do you think the author of this book was thinking? If his suggestions are crazy, why did he write the book?

GLOSSARY

manuscript (MAN-yuh-skript)—the original copy of a book before it has been printed

raft (RAFT)—a flat structure, such as a group of logs tied together, for support or transportation on water

rumored (ROO-merd)—passing information or a story that has not been proven to be true from person to person

solo (SOH-loh)—something that is done without another person

strand (STRAND)—to leave in a strange or an unfavorable place without means to leave

torpedo (tawr-PEE-doh)—a bomb shaped like a tube that is fired underwater

tread (TRED)—to keep the body nearly upright and the head above water by moving feet and hands

LEARN MORE

BOOKS

Jenner, Caryn. *Shipwreck.* DK Adventures. New York: DK, Penguin Random House, 2015.

Rizzo, Johnna. *Ocean Animals: Who's Who in the Deep Blue.* National Geographic Kids. Washington, D.C.: National Geographic, 2016.

Waxman, Laura Hamilton. *Great White Sharks.* Sharks. Mankato, MN: Amicus High Interest, Amicus Ink, 2017.

WEBSITES

Ocean Portal
kids.nationalgeographic.com/explore/ocean-portal/

Oceans for Kids
www.ducksters.com/geography/oceans.php

Smithsonian Ocean Portal
ocean.si.edu/

INDEX